Mae Jemison

Jennifer Strand

abdopublishing.com

Published by Abdo Zoom™, PO Box 398166, Minneapolis, Minnesota 55439. Copyright © 2017 by
Abdo Consulting Group, Inc. International copyrights reserved in all countries. No part of this book may be
reproduced in any form without written permission from the publisher. Abdo Zoom™ is a trademark and logo
of Abdo Consulting Group, Inc.

Printed in the United States of America, North Mankato, Minnesota
072016
092016

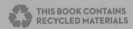
Cover Photo: NASA
Interior Photos: NASA, 1, 4–5, 6, 7, 12, 15; iStockphoto, 8, 10; Bob Galbraith/AP Images, 9; Chris O'Meara/AP Images,
13; Thom Baur/AP Images, 14–15; Dima Gavrysh/AP Images, 16; Kevin Wolf/Bayer Making Science Make Sense®/
AP Images, 17; Sandra Joseph and Kevin O'Connell/NASA, 18–19; Rene Macura/AP Images, 19

Editor: Emily Temple
Series Designer: Madeline Berger
Art Direction: Dorothy Toth

Publisher's Cataloging-in-Publication Data
Names: Strand, Jennifer, author.
Title: Mae Jemison / by Jennifer Strand.
Description: Minneapolis, MN : Abdo Zoom, [2017] | Series: Pioneering
    explorers | Includes bibliographical references and index.
Identifiers: LCCN 2016941518 | ISBN 9781680792447 (lib. bdg.) |
    ISBN 9781680794120 (ebook) | 9781680795011 (Read-to-me ebook)
Subjects: LCSH: Jemison, Mae,1956-- Juvenile literature. | African American
    women astronauts--Biography--Juvenile literature. | Astronauts--United
    States--Biography--Juvenile literature.
Classification: DDC 629.450092 [B]--dc23
LC record available at http://lccn.loc.gov/2016941518

Table of Contents

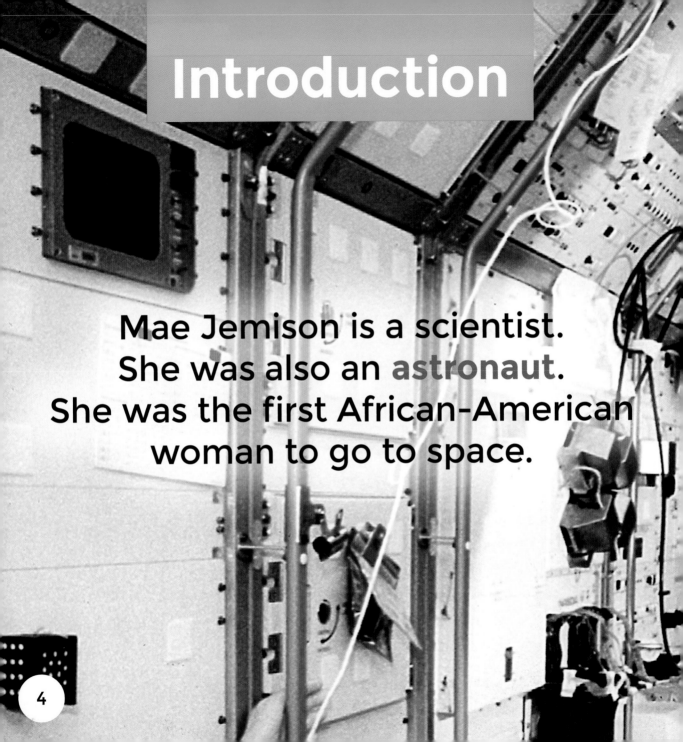

Introduction

Mae Jemison is a scientist.
She was also an **astronaut**.
She was the first African-American
woman to go to space.

Mae was born on October 17, 1956. She loved science.

She saw astronauts on TV.
It made her want to go to space.

Mae studied to become a scientist.

She read books
about space.
She also did
experiments.

9

Later she became a doctor.

Sometimes women scientists were treated unfairly. But Jemison worked hard to be successful.

In 1987 Jemison joined **NASA's** astronaut training program.

She learned
how to live
in space.

In 1992 she went into space.
She was there for eight days.

She did experiments about gravity.

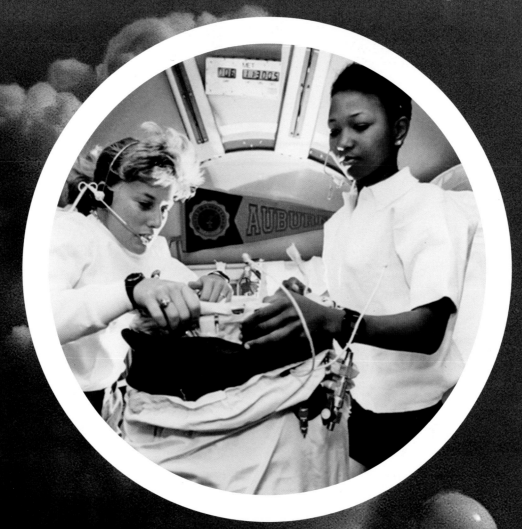

Jemison uses her fame
to help people.

She started her own company.
It uses science to solve problems.

She also started a science camp.

She works to help kids
follow their dreams.

Mae Jemison

Born: October 17, 1956

Birthplace: Decatur, Alabama

Known For: Jemison was the first African-American woman to go to space.

Key Dates

1956: Mae Carol Jemison is born on October 17.

1981: Jemison graduates from medical school.

1987: Jemison trains with NASA.

1992: Jemison goes into space on the space shuttle *Endeavour*.

1994: Jemison starts a science camp for kids.

2011: Jemison joins a team working to make a spacecraft that would go to another star.

Glossary

astronaut - someone who travels to space.

experiment - a scientific test.

gravity - a force that pulls things toward the center of the earth and keeps them from floating away.

NASA - stands for National Aeronautics and Space Administration. It leads space exploration for the United States.

Booklinks

For more information
on **Mae Jemison**, please visit
booklinks.abdopublishing.com

Zⵔm In on Biographies!

Learn even more with the Abdo Zoom
Biographies database. Check out
abdozoom.com for more information.

Index